Why Do I Look Like the Milkman, Mam?

(My Life in the Valleys, Through Rhyme)

Kelvin Smith

First published 2019
by Rowanvale Books Ltd
The Gate
Keppoch Street
Roath
Cardiff
CF24 3JW
www.rowanvalebooks.com

A CIP catalogue record for this book is available from the British Library.
ISBN: 978-1-912655-48-9

This book is dedicated
To my Mam and Dad,
Who have always been my parents,
Since I was a lad.

I owe everything to both of them,
My big ears and the wit,
And, of course, I wouldn't be here now
If the two of them hadn't done it!

CONTENTS

Foreword

They say that you never know a man until you've walked a mile in his high heels.

Well, even with a friendship that has lasted nearly fifty years, I can say that I never really knew Kelvin until I started reading his poems, odes and ditties.

What can you say about his obvious talent with words? His books have always become favourites with friends, along with friends of friends of friends.

While many of his poems have always had a "slap and tickle", tongue-in-cheek humour about them, he can also be creatively serious, especially when writing about family and friends, and all things Welsh.

He'll surely have you laughing out loud and shedding a tear, sometimes in the same poem.

I'm sure that you will enjoy this book of lyrical stories of Wales and all things Welsh, from the Maestro himself.

Steve Jones, MBE and Olympian

Former World Record holder for both the marathon and half marathon

(INTRO) – THANK YOU (MY DEAR CYMRU)

Thank you to the mountains, I climbed you
every day,
Thank you to the daffodils, how I've watched
you sway.

Thank you for my Welshness and the things I say,
Thank you for the rich soil, where my fathers lay.

Thank you for the dragon, the symbol of my pride,
Thank you to the boys in red, with the anthem I
have cried.

Thank you for my accent, the folk tales and
the rumour,
Thank you for my heritage and my sense of
humour.

Thank you for my whole life, it was you that
moulded me,
Thank you for my rhyming, without it where'd I be?

Thank you to my close ones, the laughing and
the play,
Thank you all for loving me, I loved you every day.

Thank you for the friendships, lifelong and so true,
Thank you, my dear Cymru, for my life in you.

And thank you, dear readers, I hope you have
fun times,
Remembering your Valley life, when you read
my book of rhymes.

Diolch!

WHY DO I LOOK LIKE THE MILKMAN, MAM?

Why do I look like the milkman, Mam?
And why does he look like me?
Why is the fridge full of yoghurts, Mam?
And why do we get our milk free?

Why does the milkman kiss you, Mam,
When he pops in for tea?
Why does he come when Dad's out, Mam?
And why does he have his own key?

Why is the milkman in your bedroom, Mam?
And why do you say shush to me?
Why is the milkman on top of you, Mam?
Is he trying to have a pee?

Why has the milkman got a black eye, Mam?
And why did I just see him flee?
Why is Dad wearing the milkman's cap, Mam?
And counting all his money?

Why doesn't the milkman come anymore, Mam?
And why is there no milk for our tea?
Why is the milkman limping, Mam?
Did Dad kick him in the willy?

CONEY BEACH (PORTHCAWL)

*Our holiday every year during the
miners' holidays.*

The water chute was my favourite;
We chugged up to the top,
And then so fast down the other side
I thought we'd never stop.

We splashed right through the water;
We always got soaking wet.
Then we flew high up into the sky
As we circled in a jet.

We had lots of goes on the coconut shy -
Which was never really wise
'cause the feat always seemed impossible,
We never ever won a prize.

And then onto the ghost train,
Where I always held Mam's hand tight.
Cobwebs dangled in my face
With skeletons – what a fright!

The caterpillar was lots of fun
'cause the canopy covered us.
You could kiss a girl without being caught,
Which we couldn't do on the school bus.

The smell of doughnuts filled the air
With cockles and mussels too.
Candyfloss and sticks of rock,
Our money and time just flew.

If we had a few bob left over,
We'd walk back through the night,
With a bag of chips and vinegar lips
Wow! The smell, the taste, the sight.

Then when we got back to our caravan,
With the gas lights and cup of tea,
We'd pull the bed down from inside the wall
And fall asleep listening to the sea.

WIMBERRY MOUNTAIN (PENYRHEOL)

(Reminiscing about great fun up the mountain with all my friends.)

Yellow sun,
Purple fun,
Wimberries on the hill.
Walk with kin,
Purple skin,
Stained by purple fill.

Mountain high,
Touch the sky,
Roll around the fern.
When I die,
Here I'll lie,
With the sun I'll burn.

Shadows fall,
Homeward crawl,
Sunset orange sky.
Once we're fed,
Off to bed,
Purple dragons fly.

GROESWEN

(Secondary modern school, form four, in the late 60s)

I never had a uniform
That would actually fit.
Never felt confident,
Always felt like sh*t!

Never had a good physique,
Always was too thin.
Couldn't afford Clearasil,
So squeezed my spotted skin.

Never had a satchel,
Had a duffle bag.
Never had a girlfriend,
So never had a sh*g.

Never had the bus fare,
Always had to walk.
Always told to shut up,
Not allowed to talk.

Never had a tap on the back,
Never told, "Well done!"
Secondary school stank (like me),
Never had much fun.

Summer's gone, September's sh*t
At home too by the tonne.
If I could go back, I surely would,
And make them say well done.

THE CORRIDOR OUTSIDE

(Written whilst in the Heath Hospital with a heart problem)

I can't see anything behind those curtains,
I lie and listen to the sounds;
I hear the trolley in the corridor outside
As the teapot does its rounds.

Just lying here waiting for the doctor,
I wish they'd draw the curtain back.
I hear someone cry in the corridor outside
As everything turns black.

The constant sound of a dripping tap
Echoing as it hits the sink.
I hear footsteps walking down the corridor outside
It's probably the doctor, I think.

Someone's just drawn their last breath, I hear,
And there's another one on the brink.
I'm walking with someone down the corridor
outside,
It's Jesus, I think.

ICE BLUE JEANS AND RECORDS

(As a 15-year-old living in Caerphilly)

Taken for granted castle
That I pass every day,
The tower leaning towards us,
Where we used to play.

The indoor market once buzzing,
Especially on Saturday,
Ice blue jeans and records
Made our bodies sway.

Frothy coffee in Pino's Caff,
Thought I'd be a star.
Writing silly lyric rhymes,
We thought that we'd go far.

Sunless shades on a rainy day
Cool on Castle Street.
Ice blue jeans and a polo neck,
With threadbare shoes on feet.

Hanging around street corners,
That was the thing to do.
Showing off my new record,
Not second-hand but new!

When I get home, I'll dance again,
I'm in heaven all day through,
Because my record's on full blast
And my jeans are ice blue.

WHERE THE BLUEBELLS GREW

There's a place I know
Where the bluebells grow
In a wood off Bedwas Hill.
Where the sun shines through,
Where I walked with you,
And the place where I walk still.

When I smell the dew
Through the bluebells new
The scent just fills my head.
In this blue lush land,
I can feel your hand
And hear the things you said.

Though we've pastures new
And new loved ones too,
I can't help but reminisce.
When I walked with you,
Where the bluebells grew,
We both stole our first kiss.

DON

*(My tribute to the late, great Mr Don
Braithwaite BEM for services to boxing.
With love to his wife Margaret, son Glenn
and all his family and friends.)*

What now then, my dearest Don?
Life's been hollow since you've been gone.
The day that we all said goodbye,
I didn't see one dry eye.

A good honest man, so loving and true,
A gentleman, Don - that was you.
Full of smiles and time to chat,
I assure you, Sir, we'll all miss that.

You gave so many hearts a lift,
And left a legacy, your humble gift.
The boxing world will miss you so,
But because of you, it'll grow and grow.

You wouldn't like the word legend, I'm sure,
But that's what you are, Don, lucid and pure.
You always treated everyone just the same,

Never mentioning accolades, medals or fame.

Respected, admired and loved so great,
That was you, Mr Don Braithwaite.
One thing's for sure, you haven't gone,
Because you're still in our hearts, dearest Don.

WHEN BEDROOMS WERE COLD

In days of old
When bedrooms were cold
Because we had no central heating,
I wore mittens to bed
With a hat on my head
And a tea cosy to put my feet in.

Sore noses and throats,
All covered in coats,
It's a wonder we didn't catch our death.
Blanket fluff made us choke,
While we pretended to smoke,
Expelling our visible breath.

Shivering all night,
I felt the frost bite,
And I know you'll think this is silly,
But I once ran to the loo
For a pee and a poo
And discovered icicles on my willy.

I could have throttled
My hot water bottle,
It always leaked everywhere.
I dreamt of a quilt,
With no water spilt,
And waking to dry underwear.

I used to jog on the spot
Trying to make myself hot
Before I finally jumped into bed,
Then hear Dad portraying
His famous saying,
"These are the best days of your life," he said.

WHERE ONCE THE GREEN GRASS LAY

(After watching houses being built further and further up the mountain)

The green hills are leaving now,
Gradually they fade away,
As they're replaced by red bricks
Where once the green grass lay.

The picnic spots are leaving too,
Once where folk went lazing,
With no more flowers, birds and bees
And no more cattle grazing.

Down come the trees, up go the buildings,
An ever-flowing money fountain,
The earth's turned over and foundations put in
As red bricks are pushed up the mountain.

There's a housing estate I remember,
It was a field when I was a child,
Where we used to play, having so much fun,
And where once the flowers grew wild.

What's going to happen when it's all gone?
Because it's disappearing every day.
I now look to where disasters took
What nature gave to us away.

The green hills are leaving now,
Gradually they fade away,
As they're replaced by red bricks
Where once the green grass lay.

SPITTING BLACK

Spitting black off his chest,
While his friends are laid to rest,
Scars of blue upon his face,
Because of the black he once chased.

Every day to do his graft,
Lowered down that deep black shaft.
And because of crawling on his knees,
Spitting black was his disease.

That's how he spent his every day,
Dug loads of coal for little pay.
Heaven was the glowing hearth,
Clearing the black in his tin bath.

His inner black not so easy though,
So spitting black helped it go.
A little cheese and a hunk of bread,
Too tired to climb the stairs to bed.

And when he did, sleep he'd lack,
Coughing the night, spitting black,

Which brought early death and final rest,
Buried with the black still on his chest.

THE GIRL IN THE TIGHT RED SWEATER

(Written when I was 13 years of age at Llantarnam Sec. Mod.)

The girl in the tight red sweater always makes me hot,
Coz what she's got, I'm afraid to say, sticks out an awful lot.

I'm in form one, she's in form three,
I don't think she's ever looked at me.

I can't help but stare on school days,
Especially when she turns sideways.

I think I'm in love, though I've never met her,
The form three girl in the tight red sweater.

She's very attractive and quite tall,
I always support her when she plays netball.

Now I'm in form two and she's in form four,
I don't seem to look at her anymore.

She looks different somehow, while others look
better,
The form four girl in the baggy sweater.

JUST ANOTHER FORCES SWEETHEART

(A sad story from Newport Station)

Tears at the station
Whilst waiting for your train.
I went to see you off to war
Fearing we'd never meet again.

I'd never seen you so handsome
In your khaki uniform.
I told you that my shivering
Was because of last night's storm.

We watched the train pulling in,
I couldn't help but breathe the steam.
The whistles blew inside my head
As the brakes made the wheels scream.

I begged and begged you not to go
But I knew you had to leave.
I wiped my tears once again
And tucked my hanky up your sleeve.

Everyone was crying,
I hugged your tunic tight.
"It's a long way to Tipperary,"
Murmured through the night.

I watched you all board the train,
Why did you have to fight?
I kissed you through the window,
You told me that you'd write.

I walked along beside the train
Not letting go of your hand,
I told you that I loved you,
You said things would be grand.

I knew that you were hurting too,
Although you always smiled.
I didn't have the heart to say
I was carrying our child.

I held your hand to my face,
God, I felt so low.
I ran with the train a little while,
Then I had to let you go.

I'm just another Forces sweetheart
That waved my man goodbye.

I wrote to you every week,
But you never did reply.

I prayed to God to look after you
And watch you while you roam.
We both waited for your safe return
But you never did come home.

THE PHOTO TIN

(Long before smartphones and computers, we always kept our photos in a tin; a second tin would be full of buttons.)

I opened up the photo tin
And there I found your smile.
I wondered how long it had been,
I suppose it's been a while.

I'll have to phone you up one day
Or perhaps drop you a line,
And then we can get together again
And make hay while the sun shines.

Many times I have thought that
But never got around
To arranging a meeting with you
Whenever your photo is found.

I suppose we've all done it
With good friends and our kin,
But, until then, I'll just put you
Back inside the photo tin.

DAD HAS FIXED THE TELLY

(Black and white in the 60s)

Put the empties on the doorstep,
Put fags and sweets on the slate,
Don't answer the door if the rent man calls;
The rent will have to wait.

Watered-down tomato soup,
Fill yourself with bread.
Looking forward to the black-and-white box
Whilst life is in the red.

Nothing in the pantry,
Toast and jam for tea,
Thank God for school dinners
And thank God they are free

Don't want to turn in early,
I'll be freezing in my bed,
One up, one down frustrating,
Brother's feet next to my head.

Looks like another exciting night
As Mam darns my socks.
Sat there while I'm still wearing them,
Eyes glued to the box.

Sunday night black-and-white telly
Takes ages warming up,
Don't talk while the Palladium's on
Or you're told to shut up.

The telly's gone all fuzzy;
Without it – what a dump.
Hooray! Dad has fixed it,
It just needed a good thump.

THE CHASE, THE CASE AND THE MISSUS

(Our trip up to London)

We caught the train from Ponty
To see Bradley Walsh and *The Chase*.
We only went there for one night;
You should have seen her case.

She took three dresses and four coats
And, of course, two bottles of booze.
A mirror, a hairdryer and pillows,
And why were there eight pairs of shoes?

She took her own coffee and two mugs,
With two loaves of her diet bread,
Two towels, a kettle and water
And a sheet to put onto our bed.

Enough underwear for a whole month,
An iron and extension cord.
She told me not to be so sarcastic
When I asked, "Where's the ironing board?"

I only took one shirt and underpants,
Some socks and the odd knick-knack.
I ended up carrying her bloody suitcase
While she carried my small rucksack.

Don't start me on our hotel room,
She filled every wardrobe and drawer,
While I hung my one shirt and jacket
On the back of the bathroom door.

When we started to get ready for Bradley,
She declared she was full of despair,
She needed to rush down to New Look
Because she had nothing to wear!!!

I WALKED THE ROAD TO SWANSEA

I walked the road to Swansea
To see my true love there.
I couldn't wait to hold her,
My true love Mair, so fair.

I met a lady traveller
Where the River Tawe flows,
I gave her a penny farthing
To buy some ribbons and bows.

When I reached the sea at Mumbles,
The weather blew a gale,
I saw a ship a-sailing
And heard a maiden wail.

I ran to the little white cottage
Where I expected my true love to be.
My heart was beating like a drum
Would sweet Mair marry me?

A little old lady answered the door;

It was my true love's mother.
She said that Mair had sailed that morn
And was taken by another.

I felt my heart crack in two,
My Mair had gone, my tears flew,
I just didn't know what to do,
Oh sweetheart Mair, I so love you.

I threw the ribbons into the sea
And watched them float away.
I gazed till they were out of sight,
God, I hurt that day.

I walked the road from Swansea
With tears, fret and prayer.
All I've done since is pine for her –
My true love, Mair so fair.

I'M A TAFF (ST DAVID'S DAY)

Up the mountains high, down the valleys low,
Lots of terraced houses standing in a row.

Pigeon cotes on the hillside, sheep by every stream,
Every town has a choir that sings for its rugby team.

Red shirts on a green field, such a thrill to see,
Must ruck and run and hit them and beat the
enemy.

Dragons every flagpole, patriotically flying high,
Anthems at the Principality can make a grown
man cry.

Ghost mines full of memories, like the castles
and the moat,
Daffodils every roadside and leeks on every coat.

Children all in costume, come assembly they will
sing,
Ballads, songs and poems, the warmth of Wales
they bring.

A little nation we may be, but I will shout aloud
From the mountain, "I'm a Taff!", and of that I'm
very proud.

YOU'LL GROW INTO THEM!

(Remember being told that? Ha!)

When I was a kid my clothes were too big,
The sizes were always wrong.
My jacket actually fitted my dad
And my trousers were far too long.

I always asked my parents, "Why?"
And they would always say,
"Don't worry, you'll grow into them."
How I longed for that grow-into-them-day.

And when that day finally came
Because I had grown so tall,
I went from one extreme to another
Because my clothes started getting too small.

So for only a couple of weeks as a kid
My clothes did actually fit,
And as for the rest of my childhood, I remember,
I walked around like a bag of sh*t.

THE LADY ON THE CORNER
(STOOD OUTSIDE THE SPAR)

There's a lady on the corner,
She always looks so smart.
I can't help looking at her
With her legs wide apart.

You must have seen her waiting there,
She stands outside the Spar.
She always seems to get a lift
From a different coloured car.

She always wears black stockings
With very high-heeled shoes,
And when she wears her short-sleeve dress,
You can see all her tattoos.

She always seems so friendly,
She's always got a smile,
Though she has a few teeth missing
And it doesn't fit her style.

One night I said, "Good evening."
She answered, "Hello young man,"
Then quickly brushed right past me
To an awaiting baker's van.

I remember one Good Friday
She asked, "Is that a gun?"
She was pointing to my pocket,
Where I kept my hot cross bun.

I asked her what her name was,
She said it was Yvonne,
But she said I could use her real name,
Which happened to be Ron.

She offered me a bit of fun
And said she'd do it cheap,
I kept on thinking, Ron? Ron? Ron?
No wonder her voice is deep!

I ran home and told my father,
But being a hard-working man,
He had to rush down to the Spar
To deliver bread in his van.

THE CHAPEL IN OUR STREET

They used to congregate
Once through the gate
With hallelujahs and a prayer.
Now unabashed,
With windows all smashed,
No one seems to care.

There was many a grapple
With the fate of our chapel,
That stood proud in our street.
Barry and Porthcawl
Were an absolute ball
When we went for our Sunday School treat.

The Valleys opposed
The chapel's now closed,
All rejected, dank and bare.
The sermon signposts
Are only for ghosts,
I wonder if God's still in there.

We were all blessed

In our Sunday best,
I sang at the top of my voice.
We were made to go
But we didn't know
It would die when we had a choice.

Now the karate boys meet
At the chapel in our street
Under ceilings all covered in moss.
No more prayers said now
And no heads bow
Yet Christ still looks down from the cross.

REMEMBERING ABERFAN

Please bless the children that once ran
Through the streets of Aberfan.
Off to school and their classroom,
Till that day of doom and gloom.

The tip that slid down that mountainside
Brought so much grief; the whole world cried.
Their lessons had only just begun,
Shattering the lives of everyone.

Through their devastating holocaust,
They searched for the babies that were lost.
When the whistles blew, there wasn't a sound,
Just tears and black slurry all around.

They waited, helpless, for any news,
How is it that God can choose?
Now millions of tears every day,
Still trickle down where children lay.

Little children, little faces, little lives.

Whatever the politics, fault or blame,
Please remember the children all by name.
Every loved child from every class,
From that dear little school in Pantglas.

Coal was life, yet it brought death.
It took away the very last breath
Of children and teachers, devastating lives,
Of mothers and fathers, husbands and wives.

Brothers and sisters, granddad and nan,
It broke every heart in Aberfan.
Another year passes, another sunset,
Please tell their story, please never forget.

Tell every woman, tell every man,
About the dear children of Aberfan.
And now all those little angels that once ran,
Fly through the white arches at Aberfan.

Innocent children, innocent faces, innocent lives.

All children bright and beautiful,
Each one so special and small.
May God bless every one of you
And catch you should you fall.

BECAUSE I LOVE HER

(My loving, passionate, ardent land.
Written whilst on holiday in Tenby.)

To walk upon the very sand
Of my loving, passionate, ardent land,
I often wonder, was she planned?
Because I love her.

A world that waits outside my door
To pick up trinkets washed ashore,
Coloured glass, my thoughts and more,
Because I love her.

To see a lonesome sparkling shell
As the waves turn like a carousel,
I drift amongst her haunting spell
Because I love her.

I breathe the winds that brush my face
That forever in time my heart will chase,
Till the sun and moon collide in space,
Because I love her.

I feel the sand between my toes;
It lifts my soul from all its woes
And banishes worries, cares and foes
Because I love her.

The birds fly close and play their game,
The ocean spirits call my name,
Our reasons for being here are all the same
Because we love her.

The clouds may rain, the sun may shine
Upon my Shangri-La, my shrine,
May all our hopes and dreams entwine
Because we'll always love her.

From my sunrise to my sundown,
She'll raise my smile and dispel my frown.
I will always stroll this hallowed ground
Because I love her.

BAGS AND SAGS AND BINGO WINGS

(When I worked at the university in Pontypridd, I was the only male in the department, and this poem tells of the regular women's conversations I endured during tea breaks – ha!)

My face has developed wear and tear,
My teeth fell out with thinning hair.
My boobs went south, my waist got higher,
My age gets lower because I'm a liar.
My chins are double, my knees just ache,
I seldom love and, if I did, I'd fake.
My skin is loose, my clothes are tighter,
And my thinning hair is getting whiter.
My telly's louder because I turn it up,
I used to gulp, but now I sup.
I cannot read without my glasses,
I envy girls with tighter arses.
It seems to be what old age brings,
Like bags and sags and bingo wings.

I used to pull men when I was a dolly,
But all I pull now is a shopping trolley.
I used to sway my hips with pride,
I dare not now, they're far too wide.
My cleavage too, where did it go?
And the spring in my step, I walk so slow.
But I'm still that young girl deep inside,
The dashing blonde, the blushing bride.
The leggy lass when whistles came,
When being young was just a game.
And when I fall asleep tonight,
I'll dream I'm twenty and my arse is tight.
And I'll reminisce all those naughty flings,
And forget my bags and sags and bingo wings.

BECAUSE YOU ARE OUR LEGEND

(My tribute to my dear friend, Steve Jones
MBE for services to running.
And to his wife Annette too, whom it's said
deserves a medal for putting up with him)

We've witnessed you triumph a thousand times
With many missed heartbeats and patriotic rhymes,
We still boast of you over beers and wines
Because you are our legend.

From these sacred hills we've all watched you grow,
Crown of undisputed champion we now bestow.
We love you more than you'll ever know
Because you are our legend.

You sprang from the loins of this great place
Born with gusto and a smile on your face,
The world soon recognised your talent and grace
And you became our legend.

With world records and titles, we've all been
enthralled,
The dragon inside you conquering all,
In "Hen Wlad Fy Nhadau", your name shall walk tall
Because you are our legend.

May your statue cast shadows and silhouettes
Long after all our final sunsets,
Your prowess forever we'll be in your debts
Because you are our legend.

So humble and true and tough to the core,
Your name shall be remembered in Welsh folklore
Faming you as an icon forever more
Because you are our legend…

Yes, you'll always be our legend.

WHEN I WAS A KID

(With Dad)

When I was a kid ,we walked some miles,
Crossing fields and over stiles.
Climbing mountains to the top,
Hoping and longing for Dad to stop.
Whoever knew what was in his head,
"Onward, men," is what he said.
Only then he'd up the pace,
Faster and faster, he'd rant and race.
Then suddenly he'd stop and wait
By that crooked gate and chew some grass till I
caught up.

He'd smile at me, sweat on his brow,
And say, "It won't be much longer now."
Then off we'd go for another mile or so,
Down a country lane at full flow.

And then the sight I'd longed to see,
That country pub staring down at me.
My sandy throat would soon be quenched,

With a shandy bloat, my face all drenched.
The bubbles made me jump with sighs,
While I ate my crisps with watery eyes.
The hiccups always made me frown,
But still I'd always gulp it down,
Because I was never satisfied.

The journey home was slow but fun,
Dad held a stick just like a gun,
That he shot at me with such a crack,
I lunged at him and fired back.
I shot him down with just one round,
And he fell backwards to the ground.
I took his gun and checked him out,
But Dad was sneaky and messed about.
He grabbed at me with playful fight,
His smell of stout wore us both out.

One day we lay for quite a while,
Dad fell asleep just by the stile.
It took him a while before he woke,
And when he did, the first words he spoke
Were of his days as a kid,
And all the things he said and did,
Yet all his hardships he still hid.

My legs would ache on the homeward track,

So Dad would carry me piggyback.
Through the ferns and down the hill,
It's all so vivid to me still.
I'd fall asleep but still hang on,
Sometimes my dad would sing a song
Of having no worries and no cares,
All the way home and up the stairs.
And as I dozed I'd take a peek,
'Twas then he'd always kiss my cheek and say,
"Love you."

OUTSIDE LOO

(60s Style)

Outside loos aren't much fun
If you only have the one, and not the two,
And the one you have
Is an outside loo.

When the snow is upon us,
The mist, the fog,
It's a ten-yard dash
To the outside bog.

You've got to be bold when the seat is cold,
With a draught howling under the door.
It's not nice trying to crack the ice,
The rebounds make you raw.

Sitting here dreaming of an inside loo,
With fitted carpets and curtains too.
It must be heaven to have a warm radiator,
And wiping your bum with soft pink paper.

Back to reality and the cold night air,
Rubbing my legs that freeze while bare.
I force myself to be accurate and quick,
While I hold the door shut and grip the red brick.

Then grab the newspaper from behind the pipe,
A quick read first, then the fold and a wipe.
I'd love an inside loo, with a fragrant smell,
But for now I'll pull the chain and run like hell.

GAPS BETWEEN OUR PILLOWS

(A woman's voice)

Gaps between our pillows
The bed has an imaginary line,
You sleep in your own half
And I'll curl up in mine.

Silence at the table,
Noticing habits now,
At least we used to talk to each other
When we had a row.

You stay out all hours,
I stay in and cry,
You don't answer my questions
When I ask where, who and why?

Pushed past in the hallway,
Saw the other side of you.
I've become a window
That you just look right through.

No more hugs and kisses,
Can't bear the thought of you,
Hatred grows more each day
When once our love just grew.

Photos in the bedroom,
Happiness we once shared.
I'm so lonely with you,
My future makes me scared.

Our home is just a house now,
No atmosphere, love or life,
All I ever wanted was your love
All you wanted was a wife.

The sink is full of dishes,
You never take your turn,
You still think you can thrust inside me
When your urges yearn.

Your breath smells of alcohol,
Our precious money spent.
Turn the heating off again,
Can't afford the rent.

Gaps between our pillows,
Crying through the night.

So near you, yet so far away,
Yet leaving doesn't seem right.

Gaps between our pillows,
The bed has an imaginary line.
You sleep in your own half again
And I'll curl up in mine.

MEGAN

Megan was a treasure,
The laughter and the glory.
When I think of Megan,
There'll always be a story.

Megan left a while ago,
We asked so many whys.
Taken away so suddenly,
No kisses or goodbyes.

But Megan surely lives on,
I know she's deep inside.
She visits me in my thoughts
And in her I still confide.

Megan lived life to the full,
She always had a smile.
Even though she hurt inside,
That was Megan's style.

Megan was the summer day,
She was the golden sun.

She is the memories on our lips,
Still loved by everyone.

Megan was quite unique,
There'll never be another.
Megan still lives in my heart
'cause Megan was my mother.

UTOPIA

It's utopia here in Cymru,
Streams of sunlight never stop.
The mountains come down to meet us
And take us to the top.

One hill nearer heaven,
The breeze within my lungs.
I can hear voices in the distance;
The wind is talking tongues.

Angels arrive above us
Through perforations in the sky.
They've come to meet us like the hills,
Adjacent, yet so high.

We reach right out to touch them,
But they rise and slip away.
As we watch them getting smaller,
From heaven where we lay.

DEAR FRIENDS

Lots of things have passed me by,
Lots of souls have made me cry,
Lots of folk have deserted me,
And there'll be more, I can guarantee.

Because people come and promises go;
One day you're high, the next you're low.
But I have come to understand,
I can count my friends upon one hand.

Whether you're near or far away,
You're in my thoughts every day.
Friendships age like a fine champagne,
And love is linked like a daisy chain.

And should I not get to say goodbye
Just like you, I'm sure to cry.
And should this day be my final end,
Then thank you for being my dear friend.

This poem is about the nicknames of all the Dais that live in the Valleys. Because there are so many Dais about, they've been given nicknames to distinguish one from another. Nicknames like Dai Twice, because his name was David David; Dai Up and Down, because he had one leg longer than the other; Dai Lamppost, because he had a lamppost right outside his house; and Dai Quiet Wedding, because he got married in slippers as he had bad feet, etc. etc.

DAI

I was stopped by a bloke in Cilfynydd
Who was from over the bridge, you see,
He said, "Can you tell me where Dai lives, good man?"
How dull can an Englishman be?

I said, "Well I'll tell you now in a minute,
I'll have to have a think about this."
I thought I'd have some fun first, mun,
So decided I'd take the p*ss.

I said, "Well there's Dai the Coal and Dai the Fish
And Dai the Corner Shop,
There's Dai who lives at the bottom of the street
And Dai who lives at the top.

"There's Dai Hand-in-the-Till and Dai the Stink,
Dai the Girlo, whose house is pink,
Dai the Parkie and Dai the Kink,
Dai with the bad eye (Dai the Wink).

"There's Dai the Cruise and Dai the Booze,
Dai the Nutter and Dai Red Shoes,
Dai the Giro, Dai Annoy,
Dai the Winky and Dai Big Boy!

"There's Dai the Scruff and Dai Bald Head
And Dai Who-Ate-All-the-Pies.
Dai the Brag and Dai the Slag
And Dull Dai (with open flies).

"There's Dai Sick Note and Dai the Laugh,
Dai the Scrap and Dai Outside Half.

Dai the Liar, Dai the Bus
And Dai the Gob, who likes to cuss.

"There's Dai Tip Toes and Dai the Bread,
Dai the Stunt, who's almost dead.
There's Weird Dai and Dai the Shaker,
And Dai Death, the undertaker.

"Dai Nine Kids and Dai the Dance,
Posh Suit Dai and Dai Tight Pants."
I could have gone on about Dai the Song,
But he interrupted me with, "Is this going to take
long?"

"Hurry up," he said. "There's a good chap,
We're supposed to be meeting for lunch."
So I sent the posh git to Heol Nant
Where I knew he'd find Dai the Punch!

DAD

Dad! Where are you, Dad?
Can you hear me call your name?
Let me see you for just a minute, Dad,
Do you still look just the same?

Oh come on Dad, just a quick cwtch
And then I'll let you be.
Just a wave or whistle a song,
Please come back and visit me.

Dad! Where are you, Dad?
Are you on that shining star?
Are you really up in Heaven, Dad?
Please tell me where you are.

I watched the game alone last week,
You would have loved it, Dad – we won!
I miss you shouting, "Come on Wales!"
It was fantastic being your son.

Dad, I sometimes smell your aftershave,
When I picture you, I'm glad

For the time before Jesus took you
That you spent with me as Dad.

Dad, since you left Mam's been ill
And I've been very sad.
Please visit me in my dreams,
I love and miss you Dad.

A SPERM'S DESTINY

(Don't ask!)

I'm just an ordinary swimming sperm
Out to reach the eggs,
Hoping one day I'll walk about
With a body, arms and legs.

There are millions of us, I'm sad to say,
Praying, "Please make it be me."
So for millions of us every Saturday night
It's just like a lottery.

That's all I've ever thought of,
It is my destiny,
To become a little girl or boy
With a Mam to cwtch-up me.

I've been hanging around all my sperm life,
My turn has come today,
As I'm thrust out fast from my man
As we both go all the way.

But it seems my days are numbered,
I didn't get very far.
I'm just a stain on a satin dress
On the back seat of a car!

SNEGGY FAIR

(My annual trek up to Senghenydd Fair)

Up to Sneggy Fair I go
Now that summer's here.
I run as fast as I can
When she visits every year.

Her face is always shining,
Her feet are always bare,
Romani belle will be waiting for me
When I get to Sneggy Fair.

We'll hold hands once again,
Non-stop through the day,
Just young fun in the summer sun
Where we'll cwtch and kiss and play.

Then when our sun decides to set,
I know my heart will tear,
Because Romani belle will bid farewell
And so will Sneggy Fair.

WE ONLY WENT THERE TO PLAY

Don't cross over the farmer's fence,
Too many rules caused us suspense,
That summer day didn't make much sense,
We only went there to play.

We knew the farmer was very mean,
So we hid in the grass till he had been,
Like soldiers we crawled in the yellow sheen,
We only went there to play.

But boys I suppose will be boys,
And over the fence, trees were toys,
While Jacko the dog was our decoy,
That day we went there to play.

So, Gerald, Christopher, Bobby and me
Climbed over the fence and climbed that tree,
Whilst Jacko the dog was allowed to run free,
He only wanted to play.

He playfully chased sheep down the track,
We heard the farmer's twelve-bore crack,
We scarpered over the fence and back,
We only wanted to play.

Jacko the dog lay dead and still,
The farmer's gun had made his blood spill,
We cried all the way home, down the hill,
We only went there to play.

THE PARK

*(My weekly rant in Morgan Jones park,
training with Phil and the boys.)*

The park's there for the children,
A safe place every day,
Somewhere to slide, see-saw and swing
As they hop and skip and play.

The park is there for everyone,
Under the sky so blue,
Round and around the fields we run
All summer and winter too.

The park's there for the old folk
A bench where they can sit.
So why do some people tend to think
It's a place for dogs to sh*t?

Just a quick rant on this page
As in the sun I nap.
Yes, I know you all clean it up,
So who left all this crap?

A FEW SMALL DITTIES…

THE AUTUMN LEAF

A leaf fell onto my head today,
As I walked across Oxwich Bay.

You may well think that's nothing new,
Because that's what leaves tend to do.

But the leaf that fell down onto me,
Was still attached to the bloody tree.
(Ouch!)

THE FOKKERS

They wanted to take everything from us
So they sent the fokkers to bomb us.
They bombed Bedwas square
And while they were there,
Thought they may as well bomb Trethomas.

WHEN YOU'VE GOT NO MONEY

(Have you ever done this?)

When times are hard
And you haven't a prayer,
When you've got no money
And life seems unfair,

Your pockets are empty,
The cupboards are bare,
Go and have a look,
Down the side of the chair!

WHY DOES MAM ALWAYS SHOUT?

Why does Mam always shout?
Why does Dad always fart?
Why did they go and separate
And break everyone's hearts?

I just hate the way that they
Correct us all day every day,
When they do far worse things themselves
Than we'd ever do or say.

Why did they ever get married?
All that pomp and fuss,
Promising, "till death do us part,"
And then gave birth to us.

They must have loved each other once
But probably just at the start,
Long before us kids came along
And the shouting and the fart!

SAD FAREWELL

(Last moments of a Welsh exile)

She looked so weak and weary,
She had no strength at all,
She didn't have much time left
When the family came to call.

So frail and pale in her bed,
No strength to even smile,
They knew it was just a matter of time,
She'd pass in a little while.

They all surrounded her with love,
So many tears flew,
Her eyes moved from face to face
As their fears grew and grew.

She tried to talk several times
And kept looking towards the door,
They queued to give her one last kiss,
But it seemed she wanted more.

Because in her eyes she was far away,

For so long she'd been out of sorts,
She hadn't smiled for quite a while,
They all wondered about her thoughts.

She stared at all the flowers
That filled both her windowsills,
And then she smiled with her last breath
When her friend brought daffodils.

DAY TRIP TO BARRY

(Silly names)

Let's all catch the Barry train
To the beach and home again.
And if it rains,
Silly names, choo-choo!

Let's all run down to the sand,
Take a paddle, hold Dad's hand.
And if it rains,
Silly names, donkey.

Playing games of silly names
When it's not so sunny.
Who will win and make us grin?
Shouting names - so funny.

Let's dig a hole with my spade,
Then show Mam what we made.
And if it rains,
Silly names, bucket!

Then at the end of our special day,
On the way home we will play.
And if it rains,
Silly names, wee! Wee!

THE BLACK BROOK

*(Named because of the black coal dust
that once coloured it.
It now runs beautiful and clear.)*

I played in the black brook too,
I once told my sons,
As they skipped stones across her
And done the things I'd done.

My dad played in the black brook too
And his dad in his day,
Paddling in the coal dust there;
It just seems like yesterday.

We'll go there soon and reminisce,
Now clear waters run,
And I'll tell you loads of stories
I promised my grandson.

LOVE HURTS

(Love at first sight as a 17-year-old, at the Double Diamond Club, Caerphilly, in the early seventies)

She looked so sexy in her leathers
As she stood up by the bar,
I couldn't resist when she tempted me with
"I don't live very far."

So we hit the cold winter's night,
Her hands were everywhere,
As soon as she opened her front door,
She was dragging me up the stair.

She led me to her bedroom,
I was full of hope,
Until she started to blindfold me
And tied me up with rope.

She whipped me hard across the chest
Then demanded that I tell
Why I didn't seem to enjoy it
And why I wouldn't swell.

"Oh let's change places," I cried out.
"You've made me rather sore."
So she eagerly let me tie and blindfold her
Then I slipped out through the door!

SITTING ON A CHAIR

(How I see myself when I pass on)

Sitting on a chair
In the middle of the air
Watching you all go by.
I feel blue
Because I can see you
But I'm not supposed to cry.

You're not allowed to see
The invisible me
As I look down on you.
So near yet far,
Your shining star
But what am I to do?

I watch you all day
And hear all you say,
While I'm sitting way up here,
Remembering good times
And silly rhymes,
What loving days they were.

Sitting on a chair
In the middle of the air
Watching you all go by.
I feel your pain
And, should it rain,
It's just the tears I cry.

CWTCH AND A WELSH CAKE

(Off my Aunty Olive)

You always made me Welsh cakes,
They always tasted yum.
There was always a cwtch and a Welsh cake,
Life was never glum.

Your ice slice was very nice,
You just couldn't get better.
It's just like saying water's wet,
You can't get any wetter.

If dreams came true, I'd be with you,
And tomorrow I'd awake,
To love so pure and laughs for sure
With a big cwtch and a Welsh cake.

(Ice slices are more often than not called custard slices these days.)

LAUGHTER

Come on, let's have a chuckle,
We need a giggle or two,
Come and have a laugh with me
And I will laugh with you.

Laughter's good for the soul,
It'll make you feel so free.
It can even take away your pain
And it can make you want to pee!

From Middle Mouse to Flat Holm
And in every village and town,
In this land of song, you can't go wrong,
So laugh and rid your frown.

Whether you laugh quite quietly
Or whether you laugh aloud,
It doesn't cost a penny
When alone or in a crowd.

So come on, let's pull some faces,
Let's blow a raspberry or two.

Just open your mouth and let it out,
That's all you have to do.

We were born with wit and banter,
It's a Welsh thing, our birthright,
So have a laugh and rid your hurt,
There's not a better sight.

Sod politics and the cutbacks
Inflation and the crime,
Just shout out loud, "I'm blessed to be Welsh,"
From morning till bedtime.

Just remember your heritage,
And if you think you're going to cry,
Just laugh and be grateful that you'll be Welsh
Until the day you die.

There's laughter in a good joke
And in a story too,
And in Wales we have fun and folklore,
So let's laugh our whole lives through.

YESTERYEAR

Milk in churns, hide in ferns,
Lovely Tizer pop,
Nylon sheets, humbug sweets
From the corner shop.

Sheepdog Lassie – Hopalong Cassidy,
Waiting for jelly to set,
Our pursuit was to catch a newt
In a bamboo fishing net.

A rare holiday at Cardigan Bay
Live on chips all week.
Tank tops and chocolate drops,
Playing hide and seek.

Desperate Dan's chin, Rin Tin Tin,
The Beano and The Dandy.
Short back and sides – fairground rides
With a bag of crisps and shandy.

Compendium of games – nicknames,
Friends that always share.

Loads of sun, a summer of fun
And not a single care.

HER AND HER DIETS

She's always on about the pounds she's shedding
Just to get into that dress for her sister's wedding,
All the different diets are doing my head in –
Her and her diets.

Shopping these days is a total riot,
Any new fads and she will buy it
And the cabbage diet! (Well, she used to fart
quiet) –
Her and her diets.

She started drinking prune juice straight from the
can,
Sunday lunch now is a bowl of bran,
So Sunday nights she'll pebble-dash the pan –
Her and her diets.

We used to have fun and chocolate cakes,
Now it's one week solids, the next it's shakes,
She's crunching Ryvita from the minute she
wakes –
Her and her diets.

She stopped buying crisps and Hula Hoops
And started eating disgusting soups,
And the smell these days when she poops!
Her and her diets.

I know it's all just a woman's game
But when she's depressed, it's me she blames,
And she always expects me to eat the bloody
same –
Her and her diets.

She's bought weird herbs in weird jars
She's blown hundreds on massages and health
spas
Yet the bin's full of sweet wrappers and Mars bars!
Her and her diets.

Every week it's the same old thing,
Down at the community centre for her weigh-in,
But she never seems to lose a bloody thing –
Her and her diets.

She says she's allowed a luxury, something nice,
Two or three times a week, that's her advice!
So it's egg and chips, pizza, curry and rice!
Her and her diets.

She's too tired for sex, but it's food I miss,
And her breath really stinks when I get a kiss,
This diet nonsense is taking the p*ss –
Her and her diets.

Then came the wedding – she said she was sound,
She jumped onto the scales, where we all found
She'd only gone and gained thirteen pounds!
Her and her bloody diets!

IF I COULD ONLY HAVE
MY WAY

If I could only have my way,
You would still be here today.
Life's not like it used to be,
When you were here to cwtch with me.

Things are so much different here,
I haven't stopped crying since last year.
There's no one to teach me wrong from right,
No one to run to late at night.

No one to read me a funny rhyme,
There's nobody waiting at home time.
No one to be there when life is cruel,
I now hate walking home from school.

No one to love me and adore,
I don't seem to laugh anymore.
No more tickles, kisses and fun,
No more holidays in the sun.

No more chatting and making plans,
No more singing and holding hands.
No one to praise me when I try,
No one to wipe the tears I cry.

So if I could only have my way,
Even just for one day,
To help repair my heart that's sad,
Because I'm still pining for Mam and Dad.

This poem is about the café I often visit in Pontypridd, mainly to listen to the typical Valley gossip and chat – I love it. It has given me so much inspiration over the years, and only recently I overheard a dear old lady say to her friend as they were leaving, "I told him, Mavis, it's either me or that bloody tortoise."
Where else would you find that type of material? Ha!

THE PRINCE'S RESTAURANT

(Cheers Bill)

I caught the bus to Ponty
And visited the Prince's Caff.
I had a joke with familiar folk,
You've got to have a laugh.

A frothy coffee and two toast,
Art deco on the wall,

I think of friends once sat with me
As their faces I recall.

Laughter and chat fill the air,
With stories that make you smile.
I sit and listen full of glee,
I love the Valleys style.

I love the Prince's Café
It's become my weekly vice,
Then while at the till paying my bill
I purchase a custard slice. Mmmm!

When I moved back to Caerphilly from Cwmbran at the age of thirteen, all the kids sang the national anthem in assembly. I'd never sung it before and didn't know the words, so I changed them, which is what I'd always done with songs on the radio and at church as a kid. One day, Mr Parry heard me and gave me the dap across the arse. I soon learned the words after that.
Here's my version as a naughty kid.

THE LAND OF MY DADS

The land of my dad's home,
Is always for me,
I'll stay here forever,
'cause Mam's here, you see.

There's not much going on here,
But it's not all that bad,

And the chip shop's quite near us,
And the pub makes Dad glad.

Glad! Glad! The pub always makes Dad so glad
It never ever closes,
Always open you see,
Come join us, we Welshmen, happy!

(Did you try singing it? Ha!)

AN OLD RUGBY CLUBMAN'S DREAM

(To Gary Crudge, former captain of Treherbert RFC)

I know I'm too old for rugby
But I just can't give it up.
Every Saturday I ask for a game,
The captain says, "Shut up!"

I won't let my arthritis stop me,
I can still jog onto the field.
I know I've got no hair and teeth left,
So no point in a gumshield.

I can still kick the odd conversion,
Who knows, I might score a try,
But the captain won't be held responsible
If I'm tackled and curl over and die.

You can put me in any position,
You can even put me out on the wing,
And I can still drink fifteen pints after the game

And I know all the songs that you sing.

Please, captain, give me one last game,
Hear an old rugger man's plea,
Let me on for just five minutes
For my kids and grandchildren to see.

Oh thank you, captain, for the game,
I'm as proud as a man can be,
Lying here in the Royal Glamorgan
With the team taking the p*ss out of me.

CWTCH

It's time to cwtch
When the weather's cold.
Give the kids a cwtch
When they're good as gold.

We all need a cwtch
When we've been hurt,
Because a cwtch is comforting
And that's a cert.

Just a loving cwtch
When you're not well,
Is better than medicine
Like a magic spell.

It's time for a cwtch
When you say goodbye,
When you fall in love
Or when a friend may cry.

You're never too butch
To have a cwtch

So cwtch up, cwtch up together,
Cwtching's a blast
That makes hearts beat fast
Cwtch up, cwtch up forever.

DAFFODILS

(My own take on the poem "Daffodils"
after being on the Brains dark)

I wandered lonely as a prat
Across the hills of Wales,
I'd drunk too much in my flat
And felt my bladder fail.
I tried my best to twti-down,
As the instant relief made me frown.

I peed for an eternity,
God I felt so ill,
I stained my trousers on one knee
And fell into some daffodils.
Too much black stuff made me unwell,
But what a beautiful daffodil smell.

I fell asleep and woke up cold
The birds were flying high up,
And just as well for me, so bold,
'cause I'd forgotten to do my fly up.
The wind was still and not a sound,

I thanked the Lord, no sheep around!

I wandered lonely as a prat
Back down those rugged hills,
I'd lost my coat and my hat
And squashed some daffodils.
And although I'd drunk more than enough,
I headed home for more black stuff.

BACK IN TIME

If I could see my future,
I don't think that I should,
But if I could go back in time
I know I surely would.

I'd love to go and visit
Those sometimes in my past,
To call on all those good times
And this time make them last.

To laugh with you all once again,
Special moments to relive,
The many times of love and fun
And this time to forgive.

There are kisses I am sure
That I'd love once again,
There are certain walks I'd take
Down a blackberry lane.

I'd love to sing you back to sleep
And watch you through the night,

I'd love to tell you those stories again
And cwtch you up so tight.

I'd love to climb those hills with Phil
We once ran every day,
I'd love to smell the bales of hay
Where we used to play.

I'd love to see JPR once more
Running from the back,
Those seventies days still amaze,
God, he took some flak.

I'd love one more of those Christmases
Running down to the festive tree,
When we were all together once,
Those times were so happy.

But the very first thing on my list,
Do you know what I would do?
I'd go back to that summer once again
And spend it all with you.

TOMMY COOPER

(My all-time favourite comedian, and of course born in Caerphilly.
Written for my grandson, for a school project about famous Valley people.)

My name is Tommy Cooper,
I was born in Caerphilly.
I'm supposed to be a magician
But I can't help being silly.

I always wear my red fez
And ruin everything I touch,
And when I finish doing a trick
I say, "Thank you very much!"

I can make things disappear
I can saw folk right in half,
And if I can't put them back together
It's okay 'cause they always laugh.

And they just keep on laughing,
All due to my simple chat,

You may wonder how I do it
Well I'll tell you – just like that!

LIFE IS SHORT

Life is short, but memories are long
The mountains will be here long after we're gone
Just like your favourite poem or song
From father to son and so it goes on.

Storms can appear on a tranquil lake
Beauty can follow after an earthquake
People are real, yet they can be fake
The world is full of hurt and heartache.

Rain is essential as well as the sun
There are different personalities inside everyone
You've not necessarily lost because you've
not won
You can still be rich when you think you've
got none.

You may well think that no one will care
You may well think there's nobody there
You may well think you haven't a prayer
But try it – it worked for me, I swear.

Yes, life is short, but the nights can be long
Sometimes it seems like it's all gone wrong
Confide in those that will make you feel strong
From mother to daughter and so it goes on.

SUNDAYS

We never had to play Mam's favourite game,
Of running behind the settee to hide.
On Sundays the insurance man never called
It was a good job no bugger died.

Dad used to file a halfpenny bit down
So the meter would think it's a bob,
Then try to convince the gasman with bluff
That it wasn't an inside job.

We ate plenty of bread with our food,
It was the way of filling us up,
I can never remember having a mug,
We always drank from a cup.

Cheese must have been cheap back in those
days
'Cause we ate a lot in our house,
Dad had it every day in his box,
How we laughed when he squeaked like a
mouse.

But my favourite day was Sunday,
Sunday dinners were always the best.
Dad would fetch some veg from the garden
In his wellies and tucked-in string vest.

We always soaked peas for our dinner,
And there were no gravy granules back then,
The cabbage was boiled until it was dead
But the flavour was ten out of ten.

We never had afters, as we called it,
But we often had trifle for tea,
Sometimes it was tinned fruit and ideal milk,
Now that was a real treat to me.

There was no such thing as lunch or brunch,
We had breakfast, dinner and tea,
And, if we were lucky, we may have got supper
But it was never a guarantee.

Yes, Sundays were always my favourite time,
A nice dinner, nice tea and then play,
And then up the wooden hill with horrible thoughts
Because it was back to horrid school the next day.

TRECCO

(Long before all the caravans had mod cons)

We found out what it feels like
To be a sardine in a can,
When the nine of us stayed in Trecco
In a four-berth caravan.

It's my turn to fetch the water
And take the bucket out,
I went and tipped last night's pee
So it's my turn for a clout.

Stuff paper in the hole in the wall,
Well that's what you've got to do,
To stop them peeping from the other side
When you go out for a poo.

Down the beach to dig up false teeth,
Dodging poo floating in the sea,
Had a clout off Dad when he found out
The poo had come from me.

Can't go to the fairground till Friday,

We've got to make the money last,
Happy memories from Trecco Bay
Now all those years have passed.

Trecco caravans now have electricity
A shower and a toilet no doubt,
But just to be sure of a Trecco atmosphere
I give all my kids a clout.

RAINBOWS, BUTTERCUPS, SONGBIRDS AND YOU

Where have all the butterflies gone?
And all the birds that sang their song?
Past glorious summers we once knew,
Where are all the fields where the buttercups
grew?

Where's the house where I used to live?
Where are all the kids I used to play with?
Where are the mountains we used to climb?
Never coming home till it was bedtime.

Rainbows, buttercups, songbirds and you,
I thought you'd be there my whole life through.
Colourful rainbows watched us play,
Kiss chase and laughing, non-stop all day.

No money or inhibitions and not a care,
Where are all the girls with ribboned hair?
I can see all your faces locked in my mind,
When life was summer, and summer was kind.

Wherever you all are, I want to be too,
To do all the things that we used to do.
Rainbows, buttercups, songbirds and you,
I thought you'd be there my whole life through.

IF YOU'RE WELSH, YOU'LL UNDERSTAND

As I look down from the mountain
At the valleys way below,
I can see the paths snake through the hills
As I watch the rivers flow.

I can see where the old pit used to be,
Where the black gold once was mined,
Black pyramids reach up to the sky
From the slag they left behind.

I can hear the church bells ringing
As they echo through my land,
They ring for God's own country;
If you're Welsh, you'll understand.

I can almost touch the clouds above
As the mist glides through the air,
I can sense the spirits by my side
With the memories that they share.

I can smell the evaporating mountain dew
As the flora swirls the skies,
I joy in the wonder of my countryside
Being a Welshman – that's my prize.

I think of the myths and legends
While the folklore drifts the hills,
I feel a shiver passing over me
Carried by the sacred chills.

The pride dwells deep inside my heart
As I breath the Welsh air in,
One day I'll be that spiritual chill
Transmitting goosebumps to my kin.

And as the dawn mist starts to clear
And the sun breaks through the cloud,
Tears start streaming down my face
Because being Welsh makes me proud.

CAN'T YOU TAKE ME WITH YOU?

Can't you take me with you?
I don't care if I die,
As long as I am with you,
I won't have to say goodbye.

Life is but a journey,
You always used to say,
So, can't I just tag along
Like a sort of castaway?

I feel like I'm a child again
And I won't have peace of mind,
So please don't leave without me.
Please don't leave me behind.

I'll only hurt without you,
It'll kill me anyway,
God, I dread tomorrow
Let's go back to yesterday.

We've come this far together,
Let's see our journey through,
Please don't leave without me,
Can't you take me too?

SANTA

*(We were always told stories about why
Santa might not come this year)*

Santa Claus lives far away
In a very cold North Pole.
He only works one night a year,
The rest he's on the dole.

He finds it hard to buy toys now,
Since they've cut his benefits.
He nearly didn't come last year
Because he had the sh*ts.

But finally, he made it,
They got him up and away,
His ingenious little elfy friends
Built a commode onto his sleigh.

PARACETAMOL CHRISTMAS

(One less for dinner, Grampy's just died)

Christmas morning, Dad's still snoring,
Last night they all had a ball,
Mam's gone next door to borrow some more
Alka-Seltzer and paracetamol.

My brother just said that Grampy's dead,
He died with a cough and a cuss.
Nan just said he's better off dead,
Away from this crappy old Christmas.

The milk's gone off, the dog's got a cough
While they all just sit there gurning.
Pheasant sounds sh*t, but Dad nicked it
And I can smell it burning.

Uncooked sprouts, the dinner has doubts,
That's something which we all agree,
The dog's got the shites, there's no Christmas
lights,
But then again, no Christmas tree.

Dad just fell, and he doesn't look well,
he landed headfirst in the hall.
Nan sent for the hearse as Dad's head gets worse
Waiting for the paracetamol.

Grampy's just gone, I waved him so-long,
Dad dressed him with his Welsh kit on,
Nana just said, there'll be more room now in bed
And one more chair to sit on.

Arguments all day, it's the Christmas way
At least all our bellies are full.
Mam's gone back next door, to borrow some more
Air freshener and paracetamol.

OUTRO – NOS DA!

Thank you for reading me all the way through,
And thank you for purchasing my book too,
But, unfortunately, it's time to say adieu –
Nos da! Nos da! Nos da!

Goodnight to the yellow setting sun,
Goodnight to all, to everyone,
It's been so lush and tidy, mun –
Nos da! Nos da! Nos da!

Goodnight to the mountains tall and steep,
God bless all the children should they weep,
May dragons protect you while you sleep –
Nos da! Nos da! Nos da!

Goodnight to the green grass ever growing,
The streams and the rivers non-stop flowing,
Creating the pride of my Cymru glowing –
Nos da! Nos da! Ta-ra!

AUTHOR PROFILE

Kelvin started writing poetry whilst at secondary school, often getting into trouble because of his schoolboy humour. But he was oblivious to the regular cane and pain dealt out for bad behaviour back in the 1960s and he accepted his poetic justice as long as he could make the other boys laugh.

Schoolboy humour soon turned into an obsession for writing, which he has continued to do so every day since. He writes about his own moods and memories within his life, along with stories he picks up listening to chat and gossip all around him in the Welsh Valleys.

Publisher Information

Rowanvale Books provides publishing services to independent authors, writers and poets all over the globe. We deliver a personal, honest and efficient service that allows authors to see their work published, while remaining in control of the process and retaining their creativity. By making publishing services available to authors in a cost-effective and ethical way, we at Rowanvale Books hope to ensure that the local, national and international community benefits from a steady stream of good quality literature.

For more information about us, our authors or our publications, please get in touch.

www.rowanvalebooks.com
info@rowanvalebooks.com

Lightning Source UK Ltd.
Milton Keynes UK
UKHW020924231019

352133UK00005B/100/P

9 781912 655489